Nonfiction Reading and Writing Workshops

Personal Narrative

Comprehension Strategy
Visualizing

Writing Focus
Personal Narrative

Program Consultants
Stephanie Harvey
Dr. P. David Pearson

Picture Credits

Cover: (bottom left) Phillip Colla/NGS, © CORBIS, courtesy Philippe Rousseau, (top left) The Granger Collection, NASA, (objects) Steven Curtis Design; page 4 Lydia Halverson, Michael Krasowitz/Getty Images; page 5 (left to right) The Granger Collection, cover design © 2002 by Bedford/St. Martin's reprinted by permission of Bedford/St. Martin's, photo: © Lewis W. Hine/Getty Images; © 1993 Carmen Lomas Garza/Photo Credit M. Lee Featheree, website © Marilyn Cangro, used by permisson, Shaun Betterill/Allsport; page 6 © Steve Prezant/Corbis; page 6–7 Lydia Halverson; page 8 (left) Library of Congress, page 8 (right) page 9, 11, 13, 14 New Bedford Whaling Museum; pages 10–11 The Granger Collection; page 12 Mariner's Museum, Newport News, VA.; page 16 Gare Thompson, Kendall Whaling Museum, Sharon, MA.; page 18 Lydia Halverson; page 19 © Royalty-Free/Corbis; pages 22–23 (top row left to right) (pencil) Steven Curtis Design, PhotoDisc®, Steven Curtis Design, Digital Vision/ Getty Images, (bottom row left to right) (comic book art) Steven Curtis Design, © Jay Schlegel/CORBIS, Steven Curtis Design; page 24 Icon art by John Haslam.

Info-Pal icon art by John Haslam.

Produced through the worldwide resources of the National Geographic Society, John M. Fahey, Jr., President and Chief Executive Officer; Gilbert M. Grosvenor, Chairman of the Board; Nina D. Hoffman, Executive Vice President and President, Books and Education Publishing Group.

Prepared by National Geographic School Publishing

Ericka Markman, Senior Vice President and President, Children's Books and Education Publishing Group; Steve Mico, Vice President, Editorial Director; Marianne Hiland, Executive Editor; Jim Hiscott, Design Manager; Kristin Hanneman, Illustrations Manager; Matt Wascavage, Manager of Publishing Services; Sean Philpotts, Production Manager.

Manufacturing and Quality Control

Christopher A. Liedel, Chief Financial Officer; Phillip L. Schlosser, Director; Clifton M. Brown, Manager

Program Consultants

Stephanie Harvey, National Educational Consultant, Colorado; Dr. P. David Pearson, Professor and Dean, University of California, Berkeley

Program Development

Mary Anne Wengel

Book Development

Morrison BookWorks

Book Design

Steven Curtis Design

Copyright ©2004 National Geographic Society

National Geographic, National Geographic School Publishing, the Yellow Border, and Reading Expeditions are registered trademarks of the National Geographic Society.

Published by the National Geographic Society
1145 17th Street, N.W.
Washington, D.C. 20036–4688

ISBN: 0-7922-4502-4

Second Printing April 2004

Printed in Canada.

For more information on the comprehension strategies used in Nonfiction Reading and Writing Workshops, see *Strategies That Work: Teaching Comprehension to Enhance Understanding* by Stephanie Harvey and Anne Goudvis. ©2000. Stenhouse Publishers, www.stenhouse.com

Contents

Part 1

Reading Workshop
Visualizing 6

Part 2

Writing Workshop
Personal Narratives 16

Extend

Introduction

Liu was confused. She looked at the list of books her teacher had given the class. "How can this be?" she asked herself. "Some of these books are stories. This one's about a girl who worked for gold miners in California. I love that book! But is that the kind of book I can use to get facts for a report? Is it a true story?"

Personal Narratives

The book Liu had read was a **personal narrative.** A personal narrative is a story about a real event told by someone who lived during that time. It includes the thoughts and feelings of the person telling the story. A personal narrative is one kind of **nonfiction.**

Sometimes an author creates the character who tells the story about the past. The author does careful research to create the character. A personal narrative, whether it is written by the person who lived the story or written by an author who invents a character to tell the story, is an exciting way to learn about the past.

All About Personal Narratives

- A personal narrative tells the story of real events.

- Personal narratives are told by a person who is in the story. They include the feelings and thoughts of that person.

- The important details are factual.

- A personal narrative looks and sounds like a story. It has a beginning, middle, and end.

In this book, you will learn the strategy of **visualizing** when you read personal narratives. You will learn how to write a personal narrative to tell about something that has happened to you.

More About Nonfiction

- Nonfiction writing provides facts—it's not made up.

- Kinds of nonfiction include documents, biographies, autobiographies, letters, reference books, and informational books.

- Nonfiction often has **features,** including maps, subheads, captions, photographs, diagrams, and words in **bold print.**

Personal narratives are personal stories about real events.

5

Part 1

Reading Workshop
Visualizing

Understand the Strategy

When you go to a movie, you see and hear what happens on the screen. Sometimes, just watching the actors, you can almost feel, taste, and smell what happens as well. Readers can do something similar when they visualize. Visualizing is using the words the author writes and what you already know to create pictures in your mind. You might think of visualizing as turning a book into a movie while you are reading.

Visualizing—Not for Readers Only

Visualizing is not just for you the reader. Think about it. A reader takes the words on a page and turns them into pictures in his or her mind. A writer takes a picture in his or her mind and thinks of the words to use to describe it. He or she thinks of words to describe sights, sounds, feelings, tastes, and smells for the reader.

Loons calling crazily

Twigs crackling

Waves slapping on the shore

Trees making weird shadows

Fingers sticky with marshmallows

Insects chirping

Smoke in my eyes

Strategy

Visualizing

Here's how to use the strategy of visualizing when you read.

- **Look for describing words** the author uses. These words will tell you how things look, taste, smell, sound, and feel.

- **Look for comparisons** you can use to paint pictures in your mind. *Does the author compare something unfamiliar to something you already know?* For example, comparing a whale to a school bus lets you picture how big a whale is.

- **Add what you already know** to what you read to create a picture in your mind.

- **Edit your mental movie.** Read on. Use the new details to "edit" the pictures in your mind. Use the new information to check your ideas.

Think As You Read

Use this routine as you read "Hunting Whales," a story written as a personal narrative. For this story, the author made up the characters, but he tells about something that really happened. "Hunting Whales" is told by Michael, a cabin boy on a whaling ship.

1 **Preview.** Read the title and the subhead. Look at the pictures. Ask yourself: *What will I be reading about?*

2 **Read the narrative one page at a time.**

3 **Think as you read.** Use words and pictures to visualize the people, places, and events you read about.

4 **Take notes as you read.** Write down the words that help you visualize. Write down questions you have or things you wonder about.

5 **Share your ideas about what you read with a partner.**

Note-taking Tool

Write on sticky notes.
Use a code:
* ***** Words that help me visualize
* **?** I have a question.
* **!** Remember this!

Note-taking Tool

Make a chart for taking notes. Write words that help you visualize. Then write what you see in your mind. Write questions and responses too.

Words That Help Me Visualize	What I See in My Mind	Questions and Responses

Visualize as you read about the whale hunt. Remember to read one page at a time. Then stop and think. Look for the words that help you make pictures in your mind. Write these down in your notes. The margin notes will help you get started.

HUNTING WHALES

We have been at sea for five weeks. Each day starts the same. Dawn breaks. Cook screams for me. I help Cook with breakfast. Then I go on deck to clean.

The officers get the whaleboat crews ready. Each whaleboat has an officer who leads them, a harpooner, and a crew of four. For three hours, the crew practices. The captain shouts, "To the boats!" The men fly to the boats and lower them. They quickly row out to sea. Waves hit the boats hard. The men return wet and tired.

Two hours later, the lookout yells, "There she blows!" A sperm whale has been spotted. The captain orders the crews to the whaleboats. Using his **spyglass**, Captain Hill locates the whale. I see her. She is huge.

The boats race toward her. Then they stop. Whales have good hearing, and noise scares them off. We all wait. Will the whale stay on the surface or dive?

The whale dives. The waves rock the whaleboats. I think that the boats are going to sink, but they don't. I hear the officers commanding the men to stay calm. Suddenly the whale looms up right beside one of the boats.

The title tells what the story will be about.

"We" refers to all the people on the whaling ship. "I" refers to Michael, the boy who tells the story.

Use these details to picture what it sounds like and what it looks like.

Put yourself in the picture. How do you feel? What do you see? Taste? Hear?

These action phrases help you picture what it was like on the whaleboat.

Practice and Apply the Strategy

Visualize what happens on these two pages. Ask yourself:
What words help me picture what it is like to be on the boat?
Have I ever experienced anything like this? How would I have felt?

These phrases help you "see" how the whale, the harpoon, and the boat move.

The men are quiet. One wrong move and they will be lost. The men in the other boats begin rowing hard to pull closer to the whale. The harpooner in the first boat raises his harpoon. He gets ready to throw. The officer commands, "Strike!" The harpoon sails into the whale. It is a hit. We cheer. But the hunt is not over.

The whale dives. The line attached to the harpoon flies out of the boat. The whale surfaces. Pulling the boat behind it, the whale races away. Pedro tells me the crew is on a "Nantucket sleigh ride." They fly across the water.

Tiring, the whale slows down. The boatsman's spear hits the whale in the lungs. It is now dying. Our first whale has been captured. Now the hard work begins.

Use this picture to add details to your visualizations about what the hunt looks like.

These words help you visualize by comparing cutting the blubber to something you know.

The tired crew tows the 50-ton whale to the ship. We have to cut up the whale quickly. Otherwise, the sharks will get it. The captain tells us that we will work in six-hour shifts day and night until the job is done. The crew ties the whale to the side of the ship with heavy chains.

Cutting platforms are set up. First, the blubber, the thick layer of fat, is cut off. The men use 15-foot long poles to cut it. Cutting blubber is like peeling an orange. The blubber is cut into long pieces, or blankets. They are very heavy.

The blankets are hauled on deck. They are then cut into small strips or "bible leaves." They look like my books. This is dangerous work. If the men fall into the water, the sharks will attack them.

▲ The crew hauls a whale aboard ship.

What happens next on the whaling ship? Use the details to help you picture what happens on the ship and then on the way home.

▲ Parts of the whale were used to make candles, perfume, umbrellas, and hoops for women's dresses.

The blubber is then boiled in big iron pots u_ it melts and turns into oil. The oil is cooled an_ put into barrels. The barrels are stored below. This whale's oil will fill about 500 barrels. We still have over 1,500 barrels to fill.

The head of the sperm whale is valuable. We separate it into three parts. From the top of the head we scoop out the purest oil, called spermaceti. Spermaceti is used for candles and hand cream. Places like Candleworks, where Granddad works, use it.

We take more oil from the whale's lower forehead. It is not as fine as spermaceti, but it is still valuable. The jaw and teeth we save for carving scrimshaw. Pedro says he will teach m_ to carve. I want to make a carving for Grandd_

When all the blubber has been taken from the whale, the crew looks for ambergris. It comes from the whale's intestine. It is used to make perfume, and it is worth $100 a pound! No wonder perfume costs so much.

Finally we have to clean up the ship. The ship_ covered with blood. The decks are slippery. W_ have to carefully wash down the ship. Sharks _ still out there.

GOING HOME

Our barrels are full. Everyone will make money. The owners will keep most of the money. Captain Hill will get the most money after the owners. The officers will get less and the crew still less. I will get the least. But we have been successful. We are a "greasy" ship! We have lots of oil.

We sail home along the coast of Africa. We cross the **equator.** The days pass. Finally we stop at a port in the Azores. It is called St. Michael's. I buy a beautiful cloth for Ma. I can't wait to get there. I have had my adventure.

A harbor in
▼ the Azores

Check Understanding

Michael never went back to the whaling ship. But he probably carried that trip in his head for a long time. What do you have in your head after reading about his trip? Can you picture a whale hunt? Look back at the notes you took as you read. Then complete the sentences below. Look at the sample to get started.

On the Whale Hunt . . .

I hear the waves slapping against the ship.

I see

I feel

I smell

I taste

Share and Respond

What do you think about Michael's story of the whale hunt? Did parts of the story remind you of anything? Take the time now to think about what you read and how you read it. Then talk things over with a partner. Ask each other questions.

- *What information was new or surprising?*
- *What did you see in your mind as you read?*
- *What do you still wonder about?*

Write a Response

Choose something that happened in the story to write about, such as the whale hunt, the harpooning, or cutting the blubber. In your response,

- Include an event from the story
- Tell how you visualized the event
- Tell what you still wonder about

Here's one reader's response.

> I liked when they cut up the whale. They tied it to the boat with heavy chains. I pictured these like the chain I lock my bicycle with but much bigger and heavier. They were probably rusty too, since they are in the water so much. My mom cut up a fish my uncle caught once. It smelled really bad. Imagine if it weighed 50 tons! Gross! They cut the blubber into strips that looked like books. I bet they looked like my grandpa's encyclopedias. I wonder why they didn't pull the whale onto the boat before cutting it up.

The writer included an event from the story.

The writer included what he visualized.

The writer tells what he wonders.

Part 2

Writing Workshop
Personal Narratives

Author's Chair

An Interview with Gare Thompson

Gare Thompson is an author of many books. He wrote a book called *A Whaling Community of the 1840s*. The story you read is from that book. We asked him some questions about his writing.

Q How did you decide to write about life on a whaling ship?

A *I live in Massachusetts. Whaling was an important industry here long ago. Whaling and whaling ships have always fascinated me. I love visiting whaling museums and reading about whalers' adventures.*

Q Why did you write this book as a story rather than as a typical nonfiction book?

A *I want kids to know that history is really one big story about people. So if I'm writing about a time long ago, I want to tell it through the eyes of someone who* lived through that time. That way, the reader gets to experience life as it was for a typical person of the time.

Q How do you make sure everything in your books are true, even if the people are made up?

A *Research, research, research! I start out as if I were going to write an article for a textbook or an encyclopedia. Then I close my eyes and think about whom I would want to be if I had lived then. Then I try to tell the story from that point of view. It's really a lot of fun to write like this.*

Gare Thompson turned what he knew about whaling into a story told by a boy on a whaling ship. You can turn one of your experiences into a **personal narrative** by following the steps on the next few pages.

Prewriting

Focus on Content and Organization

Choose Something to Write About

One good thing about a personal narrative is that you don't need to look far to find something to write about! Your personal narrative will be a true story about something that happened to *you*.

Events to Write About

Going to the new museum

The time I broke my arm

The soccer tournament

The tornado last summer

Brainstorm Words to Use

Do you know what to write about? Now close your eyes and visualize the scene. Think: *What do I see? Smell? Taste? Feel? Hear?* Write these ideas down. You can use some of them when you write.

The Tornado Last Summer				
I see	I hear	I feel	I smell	I taste

Think About the Beginning, Middle, and End

Every good story has a beginning, middle, and an end. Think about your story. Where does it begin? How does it end?

You can draw 3 pictures to help you plan your story. Sketch one for the beginning, one for the middle (or the most important or exciting part), and one for the end. What will you draw?

Here are pictures one writer sketched to plan his story.

Before the storm

During the storm

After the storm

Drafting

Focus on Voice and Word Choice

It's time to start writing. Use your pictures and all your notes as you write. Remember that you're writing a *personal* narrative. Try to sound like yourself as you write. Here's one writer's first draft.

Writing Tip

Use the story on pages 9–13 as a model. What details will you use to help your readers visualize?

When my mom and dad heard about the tornado I was down the street at my friend Toms house. They came running down to his house really fast and yelled to get home right now. I thought I was in trouble because I left my comics on the floor. My mom grabbed my hand and ran home. She kept yelling for me to hurry up a storm was coming. When we got home my mom said there was a tornado coming. I thought she was going to cry but I didn't know what a tornado was so I kept acting brave. I said "ok. can I go back and play?" She told me that a tornado was a big storm like in the Wizard of Oz. It could blow our house away.

My dad had us all get into the big closet. We heard stuff outside but then we didn't hear nothing. We went out and our house was OK. Dad said if we were at Grandma's house we would go down to the basement.

Revising and Editing

You've got your ideas down. Now it's time to think about changes you may want to make. What details can you add to help your readers visualize what you've written? Read your draft. Use the Revising Checklist to help you plan how to revise.

Last summer my parents yelled at me and made me spend an hour in a dark closet. They weren't being mean. We had a tornado!

When my mom and dad heard about the tornado I was down the street at my friend Tom's house. They came running down to his house. ~~really fast and~~ Mom yelled, to "get home right now!" I thought I was in trouble because I left my comics on the floor. # My mom grabbed my hand. ~~and ran home.~~ She kept yelled ~~yelling for me to "hurry!~~ up a storm <u>is</u> ~~was~~ coming!" When we got home, my mom said, "there <u>is</u> ~~was~~ a tornado coming." ~~I thought she was going to cry but~~ I didn't know what a tornado was so I kept acting brave. ~~I said "ok, can I go back and play?"~~ She said, ~~told me that a tornado was a~~ "Remember the big storm ~~like~~ in the Wizard of Oz.

Revising Checklist

- Do I tell about something that really happened?
- Do I have a beginning, a middle, and an end?
- Do I use pronouns like *I* and *me*?
- Do I include action phrases and details to help my reader visualize?

Add Dialogue

You may want to revise by adding dialogue. Adding what people say makes your writing sound believable. Using dialogue helps you write action scenes that are exciting to read.

Original
She kept yelling for me to hurry up a storm was coming.

Revised
She yelled, "Hurry! A storm is coming!"

Edit

Proofread your narrative. Check your spelling and punctuation. Read each sentence to make sure it is clear and interesting. Do you begin and end each sentence correctly?

Proofreading Marks

Take out	⤷	Capital letter	☰
Insert	∧	Spelling	○
Small letter	/	New paragraph	¶

Sharing and Publishing

Tell Anecdotes

When you tell a personal story in an entertaining and informal way, it is called an anecdote. Share your story by reading or telling it aloud.

Draw the Action

Choose the most exciting part of your story and illustrate it. Then read your story to a classmate and share your illustration. Does your classmate agree that you've illustrated the most exciting part of your story? Post your story and illustration where other classmates can respond to them.

Design a Magazine

With a friend, design a *zine*, or homemade magazine. You can put your personal narratives and other writing in your zine. Decorate the articles with pictures and captions and distribute copies to the class.

Extend
On Assignment

Look Back

In this book you read about personal narratives. You also learned the strategy of visualizing while you read. What would you tell Liu about personal narratives? Why do you think her teacher thinks personal narratives are OK to use to get information for history reports?

Assignment 1

Personal Narrative

When you wrote your personal narrative, you wrote about something that really happened to you. You included your own thoughts and feelings.

Your assignment: Rewrite your personal narrative. This time, write about what happened, but from the viewpoint of someone or something else that was also there. You can tell the story from the point of view of a friend, a professional athlete, your dog, the kitchen table, your bicycle— whatever!

Here's my story!

Learn More

You can use what you have learned about reading and writing to do some investigating on your own. Go "On Assignment" with one or more of the following activities.

Assignment 2

Think Visually

Readers visualize when they read. Writers visualize when they write. How about artists? They visualize too, and sometimes, they try to tell a story in a single drawing or in a few drawings.

Your assignment: Be an artist and tell a story with pictures. You might draw one picture that tells the whole story. Or you might draw a panel of pictures, as in a comic book. A comic book tells a story with pictures and few words. Each drawing moves the story forward. Think of a story you want to tell and tell it, using pictures.

Assignment 3

Map the Whaler's Route

Reread the story about hunting whales. Note that when ships left to hunt, they followed the paths of migrating whales.

Your assignment: Trace a map of the world. Look up the migration patterns of whales in an encyclopedia or science book. What route would you take to follow the path of one kind of migrating whale? Trace the route on your map. Label the oceans and seas you would travel through, as well as continents and countries you would pass along the way.

Assignment 4

A Whale of a Chart

Do people still hunt whales? Find out more about whales or whale hunting and present the facts you find in a graph or chart.

Your assignment: Research whales and/or whale hunting. Find information you think is interesting, such as how the population of sperm whales has changed over the past 200 years. Show your information on a graph. You might want to find out how long different kinds of whales are. You could show this information on a bar graph.

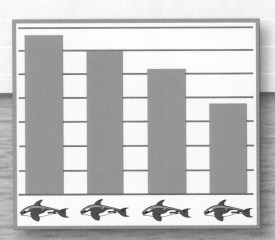

Sources You Can Use

Check out these Internet sites and books when you go "On Assignment."

The Kendall Institute—Heroes in the Ships

Explore the stories of African Americans who were on the crews of whaling ships. Examine historical journals, photographs, and paintings that span the entire history of America's whaling industry.
http://www.whalingmuseum.org/kendall/heros/index_h.html

National Wildlife Federation—Humpback Whales

Trace their migration paths, read about their history, or listen to their songs on this site all about Humpback whales.
http://www.nwf.org/keepthewildalive/whale/

New Bedford Whaling Museum

Visit the museum to learn about the history of whaling in America.
http://www.whalingmuseum.org/

Whales: Giant, Mysterious Creatures of the Sea

Read all about whales and their habitats. Discover why some whales are endangered and what is being done to protect them.
http://www.ecokidsonline.com/pub/eco_info/topics/whales/index.cfm

A Whaling Captain's Daughter: The Diary of Laura Jernegan, 1868–1871

by Laura Jernegan, edited by Megan O'Hara
Learn about day-to-day life on a whaling ship from the diary of a young girl who actually lived on one.
Blue Earth Books, 2000.

Gone A-Whaling: The Lure of the Sea and the Hunt for the Great Whale

by Jim Murphy
Read true-life accounts of the adventures and hardships faced by the young crewmembers of whaling ships, from the nineteenth century to the present day.
Clarion Books, 1998.

Hunting Neptune's Giants: True Stories of American Whaling

by Catherine Gourley
Excerpts from sailors' diaries and ship documents tell the story of whaling in 19th century America.
Millbrook Press, 1995.

Thar She Blows! Whaling in the 1860s

by Sue Kassirer
This book about the heyday of America's whaling industry is told through the eyes of a modern-day girl who finds herself suddenly transported to a whaling ship of the 1860s.
Soundprints, 1997.

Whaling Days

by Carol Carrick
This informational book explores the whaling industry in New England from its early days to its collapse.
Clarion Books, 1996.